My Friend Jesus

Etta B. Degering

Illustrated by Robert L. Berran and Manning de V. Lee

Review and Herald ®
Publishing Association
Hagerstown, MD 21740

The activity pages for each story were written by RosAnne Tetz.
She is a former kindergarten teacher, the mother of two preschoolers,
and a free-lance writer living in Silver Spring, Maryland.

03 02 01 00   10 9 8 7

Printed in U.S.A.

ISBN 0-8280-0755-1

CONTENTS

Baby Jesus

Clip——clop——clip——clop,
   went Small Donkey's hoofs
   as he s-l-o-w-l-y climbed the last hill.
Mary rode on Small Donkey's back.
Joseph walked by Small Donkey's side.
Mary and Joseph were very, very tired.
Small Donkey was tired, too.
They had come a long, long way.
From the top of the hill, O happy sight,
   they saw the lights of Bethlehem!

Joseph walked faster now.
Clip-clop, clip-clop, clip-clop, hurried Small Donkey,
    down the hill, through the gate,
    into the little town,
    where they would rest and sleep.
At the inn, Joseph asked for a room.
"We have no room," said the innkeeper.
"Is there no place where we can sleep?" asked Joseph.
"Only in the stable. . . . I am sorry."

Joseph led Small Donkey toward the stable.
He opened the creaky old door.
He held up the lantern the innkeeper gave him,
 and looked around inside.
He saw Spotted Cow, and Woolly Lamb,
 and stalls that were empty.
In one empty stall he tied Small Donkey.
In another he made a bed of straw
 for Mary and himself.
Soon they were fast asleep.

During the night the most wonderful thing happened—
    Baby Jesus was born!
Joseph filled a manger with clean new hay.
Mary wrapped the baby in soft white cloth,
    and laid Him in the manger.
The animals seemed pleased about Baby Jesus.
Spotted Cow mooed softly,
    Woolly Lamb tinkled his bell,
    and Small Donkey looked and looked.

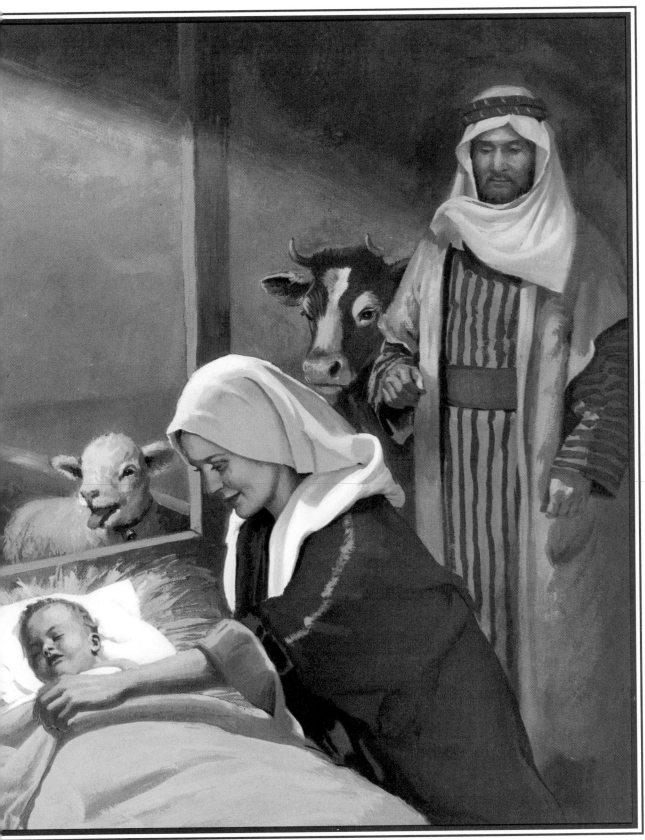

That night, in a field near the little town,
    shepherds were guarding their sheep.
Suddenly a bright light, as bright as the sun,
    shone all around them.
The shepherds were afraid
    and covered their faces.
The sheep were afraid
    and huddled together.

"Don't be afraid," said a kind, gentle voice.
The shepherds uncovered their faces.
They saw an angel, all glowing with light.
Said the angel, "I bring you good tidings of great joy!
    Jesus, your Saviour, is born.
    You will find Him lying in a manger."
Then the sky was filled with shining angels
    singing the glory song—
"*Glory to God in the highest, and on earth peace,
    good will toward men.*"

As the angels went farther and farther away,
    they looked like a twinkling bright star
    in the dark night sky above Bethlehem.
"Come," said the shepherds, "let us go see."
They ran all the way to the stable, and there
    they found Joseph and Mary and
Baby Jesus in His manger bed.

In a faraway country, Wise Men saw the angel star.
They said, "It is the star of the Baby King.
    Let us go worship Him, and take Him presents."
The Wise Men made ready their gifts.
    One Wise Man filled a bag with gold.
    Another filled a jar with frankincense,
        the perfume of flowers.
    And another filled a special box with myrrh,
        the perfume of spices.

The Wise Men gathered up their gifts,
    mounted their camels,
    and rode toward the star.
They crossed rivers and hills and sandy deserts—
    sometimes it was hot,
    sometimes it was cold,
    but always they rode on, following the star.

Then one evening the star stopped above a house
in the little town of Bethlehem.
The Wise Men made their camels kneel
in front of the house.
They climbed off the camels' humped backs,
and taking their gifts,
they knocked on the door.

Joseph opened the door—and there inside
was Mary holding Baby Jesus.
The Wise Men bowed with their faces to the floor
and worshiped the baby they called king.
They gave Him their gifts—
the bag of gold,
the jar of frankincense,
the special box of myrrh.
Then the Wise Men said good-by, mounted their camels,
and began their long journey home.

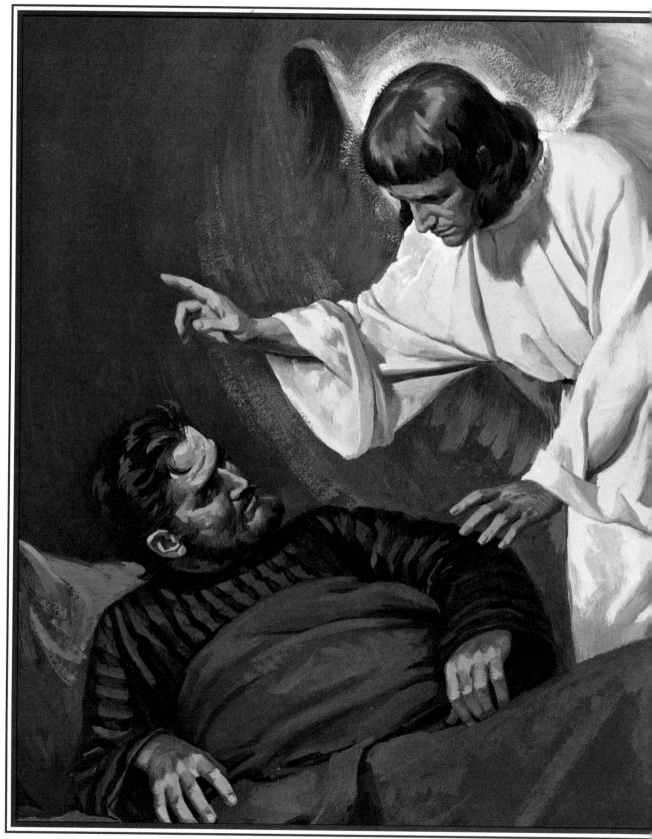

One dark night when Joseph was asleep,
and Mary was asleep,
and Baby Jesus was asleep,
an angel whispered to Joseph.
"Get up quickly," he said. "Take Mary and the Baby
and flee into Egypt. The wicked king
is trying to find the Baby to do Him harm.
Stay in Egypt until I tell you it is safe to return."
The king was angry because the people were saying
that some day Baby Jesus would be king.

Joseph got up quickly.

He told Mary what the angel had said.

He went to the stable for Small Donkey.

Mary wrapped Baby Jesus snug and warm.

Joseph helped Mary on Small Donkey's back.

He handed her Baby Jesus.

Clip-clop, clip-clop, went Small Donkey's hoofs

as they went out through Bethlehem's gate,

and turned down the road toward Egypt.

The wicked king couldn't find Baby Jesus now.

Joseph and Mary, Baby Jesus, and Small Donkey
   lived in Egypt a long time.
Baby Jesus learned to walk and to talk.
Then one night the angel again whispered to Joseph,
   "The wicked king is dead. It is safe to go home."
Once more Mary rode on Small Donkey's back,
   but the Boy Jesus didn't ride all the way now.
Sometimes He walked and helped to lead Small Donkey.
They didn't go to Bethlehem where Jesus was born.
They went to Nazareth, Joseph and Mary's old home.

Joseph and Mary were glad to be back in their old home.
Small Donkey was glad to be back in his own stable.
When Mary tucked the Boy Jesus into His own bed,
     she told Him good-night stories.
She told about—
     Baby Moses and his basket boat,
     about when the angels sang the glory song,
     about the Wise Men following the star,
     and worshiping the Baby as their king.

● Together, act out trying to find a room in Bethlehem. Close all the inside doors in the house. Get down on your hands and knees—you are the donkey. The child rides on your back. When you come to a door, the child jumps off and knocks on the door. Go from door to door. At the last door, pretend the innkeeper lets you go to his stable. Trot over there and lie down, exhausted.

● Get out the photo album. Look at your child's baby pictures together.

● Discuss why we give presents at Christmas. Think of someone you could surprise with a present today.

"Baby Jesus"

● Rock a doll in your arms and sing together "Away in a Manger."

● An angel told Mary and Joseph what to name their baby. Tell your child the story of how you chose his/her name.

● No matter what time of year it is, do something together that reminds you of Christmas: bake cookies, decorate the house in some festive way, send a card to someone.

Jesus and the Storm

Jesus stood in a boat—
    a fishing boat with oars and a sail—
    and talked to the many people
    who had come to hear Him.
All day long Jesus told them stories.
When it was evening Jesus said to His helpers,
    "Let us cross over to the other side
    of the lake and rest."

Jesus' helpers untied the boat.
They pushed it from the shore
    and raised the sail.
One man sat in the back of the boat
    to guide it with the steering tiller.
The boat moved slowly at first, and then faster
    across the quiet blue water.

A round yellow moon came up over the lake.
The stars twinkled high overhead.
Jesus was so very tired He lay down
        with His head on a pillow
        and was soon sound asleep.
The man at the back steered carefully.
The boat sailed on and on and on.

Suddenly a fierce wind began to blow.
It blew a black cloud over the moon.
It blew black clouds over the stars.
It whipped the water into huge angry waves.
The waves tossed the boat this way,
    and that way, and up and down.
There was lightning!
There was thunder!

The man at the tiller tried to steer the boat,
    but he couldn't.
Other men tried to row the boat with oars,
    but they couldn't.
Water filled the boat. It began to sink.
The men were afraid. They woke Jesus—
"Lord save us; we perish!" they cried.
Jesus heard their cry for help.
    He felt the angry wind.
    He saw the lightning flash.
    He heard the noisy thunder.

But He was not afraid.
He stood up and said to the wind and waves,
"Peace—be still."
The wind stopped blowing. The waves were still.
The clouds went away, and the stars twinkled again.
The boat sailed on the sparkling path
  that the moon made on the water,
  and crossed to the other side of the lake.
"Why were you afraid?" Jesus asked His helpers.
"Why were you afraid when I was with you?"

Jesus says to boys and girls today—
"Don't be afraid when the lightning flashes,
      and the thunder crashes,
      and the strong winds blow."
"I am with you always," says Jesus,
      "in the dark and in the storm,
I will never leave you. Don't be afraid."

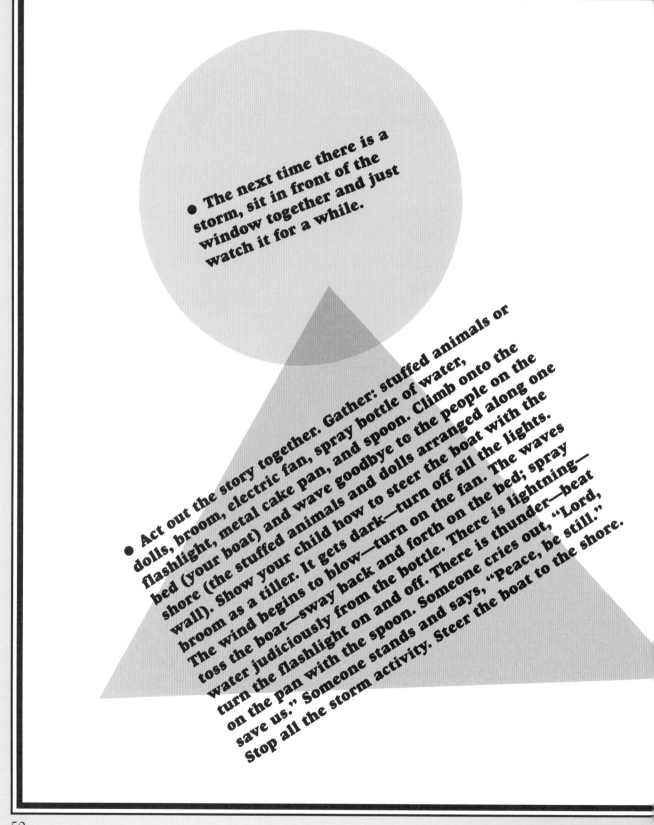

● The next time there is a storm, sit in front of the window together and just watch it for a while.

● Act out the story together. Gather: stuffed animals or dolls, broom, electric fan, spray bottle of water, flashlight, metal cake pan, and spoon. Climb onto the bed (your boat) and wave goodbye to the people on the shore (the stuffed animals and dolls arranged along one wall). Show your child how to steer the boat with the broom as a tiller. It gets dark—turn off all the lights. The wind begins to blow—turn on the fan. The waves toss the boat—sway back and forth on the bed; spray water judiciously from the bottle. There is lightning— turn the flashlight on and off. There is thunder—beat on the pan with the spoon. Someone cries out, "Lord, save us." Someone stands and says, "Peace, be still." Stop all the storm activity. Steer the boat to the shore.

"Jesus and the Storm"

● Climb into a rocking chair together and rock back and forth, back and forth. Close your eyes. Do you think this is what it feels like to rock in a boat on a lake?

● Sing together "All Night, All day, Angels Watching Over Me." Clap and sway to the rhythm.

● At bathtime, play with a little boat and make a little storm.

Jesus and the Children

Mark and Sara were waiting
    with Mother and baby Esther
    to see Jesus.
Other children were waiting with their mothers.
Jesus' helpers frowned at them—
    "Can't you see that Jesus is busy?
    He has no time for children."

Mark and Sara, and Mother with baby Esther
    turned slowly away.
Mark hung his head, and watched
    the dust of the path squish up
    between his brown toes.
Sara looked back at Jesus. A tear
    ran down her cheek.

Then they heard Jesus say to His helpers,
  "Suffer the little children to come unto me,
  and forbid them not."
All the children ran to Jesus.
Jesus took baby Esther on His lap.
He smiled and touched Sara's cheek
  where the tear had run down.
He put His hand on Mark's head.
The children took turns standing close to Jesus.
  He told them stories.

On the way home Mark whistled a happy tune.
Sara skipped ahead, and then she waited
    and took Mother's hand.
"I wish we could see Jesus every day," she said.
"Maybe," said Mother, "maybe soon
    Jesus will come to the Temple."

One day Mark and Sara
    heard people singing the hosanna song.
They ran to see why the people were singing.
They saw Jesus riding on a colt
    coming down the road.
People were laying their coats on the road
    for Him to ride over.
Boys were waving palm branches and shouting.
Girls were tossing flowers and singing.

M. de V. Lee

"May we go with Jesus?" asked Mark.

"May we?" said Sara.

Mark's father cut a palm branch for him, and
    Mother helped Sara fill a basket with flowers.

Mark waved his palm branch and shouted,
    "Hosanna to the Son of David, Hosanna, Hosanna!"

Sara tossed flowers on the road and sang,
    "Hosanna, Hosanna!"

It was like a big parade. It made Jesus happy
    to hear the children shout and sing.

The parade came to the top of a hill.
Jesus stopped the colt,
    and looked down over the hill.
The boys stopped waving
    their palm branches and looked.
The girls stopped tossing flowers and looked.
All the people stopped
    and looked down over the hill.
What did they see down over the hill?

There was a brook down over the hill,
    a sing-along, laugh-along brook,
    but they were not looking at the brook.
There was a city with a high stone wall
    down over the hill,
    but they were not looking
    at the city with the high stone wall.

They were looking at *THE TEMPLE,*
    the white marble Temple
    shining like a big snow castle
    in the afternoon sun.
Everyone, yes, everyone,
    had stopped at the top of the hill
    to look at the Temple,
    the beautiful Temple.

The next day Mark and Sara and many other children
    went with Jesus and His friends to the Temple.
But when they got there,
    the sounds coming from the Temple
    didn't sound like a Temple at all.
There was no sound of singing and praying.
It wasn't quiet-like and hush-like,
    with people tiptoeing when they walked.
Instead—there was a terrible rackety noise!

Traders had brought to the Temple
  cattle and sheep and doves
  to sell for offerings.
They shouted, "Buy cattle for your offering."
  "Buy sheep for your offering."
  "Buy doves for your offering."
Moneychangers were there, clinking their money.
It didn't seem like a Temple at all—not at all.
It was like a noisy market place.

Jesus stood in the doorway—
The cattle traders looked at Him.
The sheep traders looked at Him.
The dove traders looked at Him.
They all stopped their shouting and selling.
The moneychangers stopped clinking their money.
Everyone looked at Jesus and waited
    to see what He would do.
Jesus raised His arm. He said,
    "TAKE THESE THINGS HENCE!"

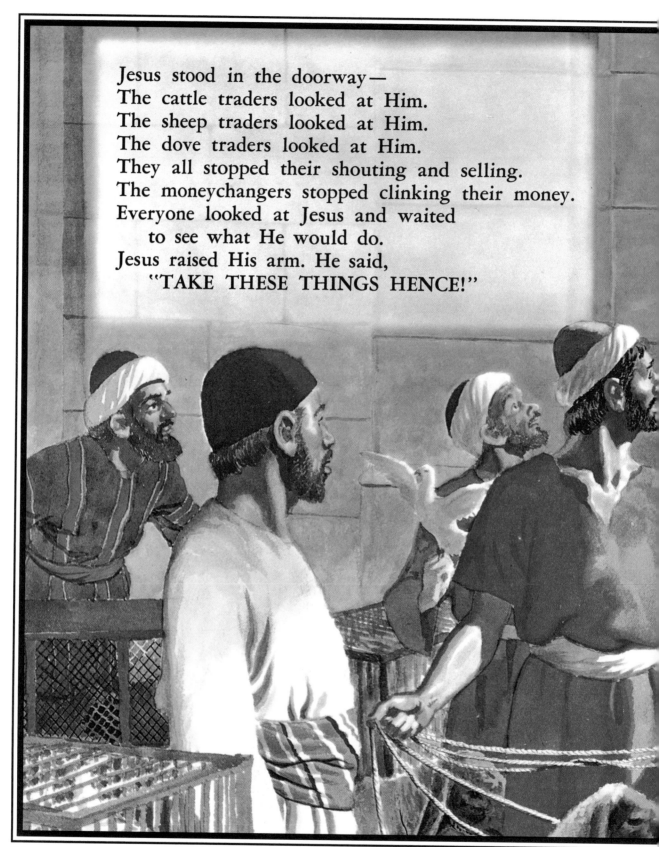

Such a hurrying and a scurrying!
The traders hustled the cattle out.
They rushed the sheep out.
They grabbed the dove cages and ran.
The moneychangers didn't even stop
    to take their money.
All the grown-up people ran away from Jesus.

But the children didn't run away from Jesus.
Mark and Sara and all the children
    crowded close around Him.
Jesus told them stories.
He took the little ones on His knee.
A little boy went to sleep on His lap.

Then the sick people came to Jesus.
A boy with a hurt leg came hobbling on crutches.
Jesus put His hand on the hurt leg
    and made it well.
The boy threw away his crutches.
Now he could walk. He could run! He could jump!

A father and mother brought
    their sick little girl to Jesus.
She was so sick they carried her in a hammock.
Jesus took her small thin hand in His. He said,
    "Be well, little girl, be well."
The little girl sat up and smiled. She was well.

A boy led a blind man to Jesus.
The blind man's eyes were tight shut.
He had never seen a tree or a house—not anything.
Jesus made his eyes see.
And the first thing the blind man ever saw
was the lovely face of Jesus.

The children were so happy
    when they saw the sick people made well,
    they again waved palm branches
    and sang the hosanna song.
The grown-up people who had run away came back.
They looked in at the Temple doors
    and heard the children singing.
They said to Jesus, "Make the children be still."
But Jesus liked to hear the children sing.
He didn't want them to be still.

It was time to close the Temple doors.
Tomorrow the children would come back
to hear more stories.
Jesus wanted them to come. He had said,
"Suffer the little children to come unto me,
and forbid them not."

Mark and Sara waved good-by to Jesus.
All the way home they sang the hosanna song,
"Hosanna to the Son of David,
Hosanna, Hosanna!"

● Take all the stuffed animals out of the toy box. Let your child shout, "Take these things hence!" and then throw them quickly into the toy box.

● Sing a praise song together, like "Praise Him, Praise Him" or "Praise Ye the Lord." If you have any palm branches, you can wave them. If not, perhaps you could make some out of cardboard or paper.

● Ask your child to pretend that he/she can't walk, is blind, or is sick. Then tell your child to act out what it feels like to be healed by Jesus.

● Build a temple out of blocks or Legos.

"Jesus and the Children"

● Go on a walk. Collect leaves and flower petals along the way. When you come back to your yard, let your child shout "Hosanna" and toss the leaves and flowers in the air.

● Snuggle with your child on your lap. Softly sing "Jesus Loves Me."

FOR SCHOOL-AGE CHILDREN
The Bible Story

This is the most accurate and complete set of children's Bible story books available. More than 400 Bible stories are included, with full color paintings at every page-opening. Unlike television, these stories introduce children to heroes you would be proud to have them imitate. These stories are also an excellent tool for loving parents who want their children to grow up making right decisions and making them with confidence. Ten volumes, hardcover.

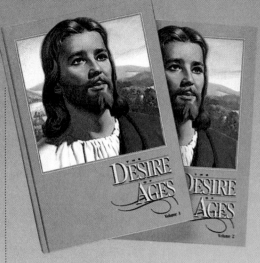

The Desire of Ages

This is E. G. White's monumental best-seller on the life of Christ. It is perhaps the most spiritually perceptive of the Saviour's biographies since the Gospel According to John. Here Jesus becomes more than a historic figure—He is the great divine-human personality set forth in a hostile world to make peace between God and man. Two volumes, hardcover.

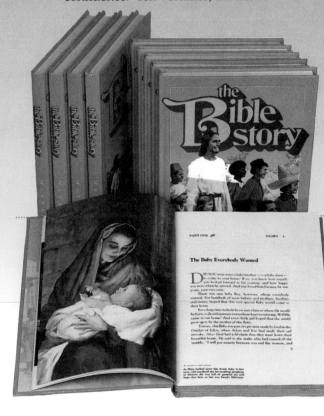

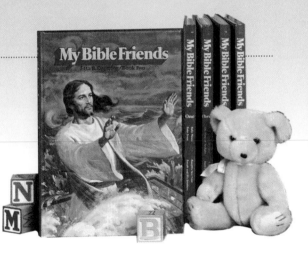

Uncle Arthur's Bedtime Stories

For years this collection of stories has been the center of cozy reading experiences between parents and children. Arthur Maxwell tells the real-life adventures of young children—adventures that teach the importance of character traits like kindness and honesty. Discover how a hollow pie taught Robert not to be greedy and how an apple pie shared by Annie saved her life. Five volumes, hardcover.

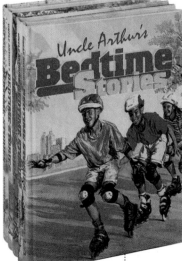

FOR PRESCHOOL CHILDREN
My Bible Friends

Imagine your child's delight as you read the charming story of Small Donkey, who carried tired Mary up the hill toward Bethlehem. Or of Zacchaeus the Cheater, who climbed a sycamore tree so he could see Jesus passing by. Each book has four attention-holding stories written in simple, crystal-clear language. And the colorful illustrations surpass in quality what you may have seen in any other children's Bible story book. Five volumes, hardcover. Also available in videos and audio cassettes.

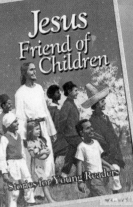
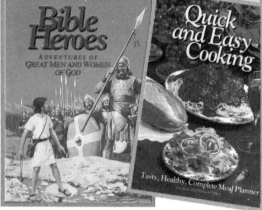